I0465665

Day Trading with Relative Strength Index (RSI)

Mastering Short-Term Profits Through Momentum
and Market Signals; Advanced Techniques for
Consistent Gains.

By

Avery Welles

Avery Welles

Avery Welles

TABLE OF CONTENTS

4

Avery Welles

Avery Welles

Introduction

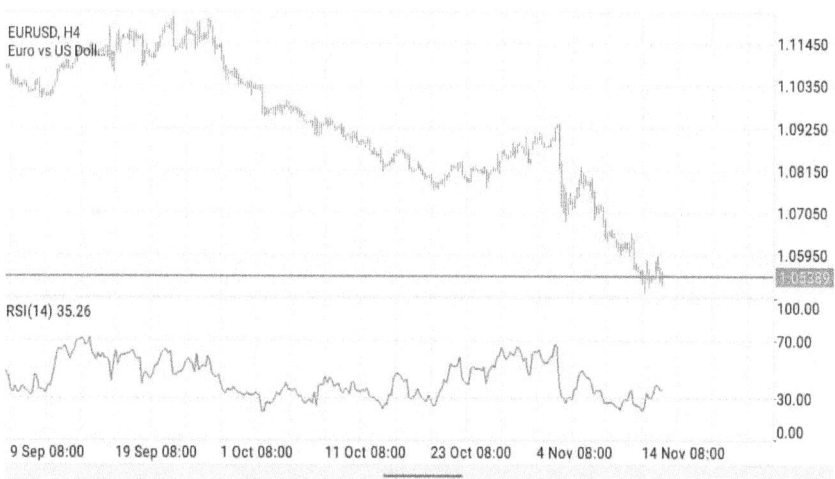

The Relative Strength Index (RSI) stands as one of the most trusted and powerful tools available to traders. Whether you're new to trading or seeking to sharpen your skills, this book provides the insights, strategies, and deep understanding you need to leverage RSI for consistent gains.

Day trading offers the allure of quick profits, but it also demands discipline, focus, and a firm grasp of market indicators. The RSI—developed by J. Welles Wilder Jr.— measures the speed and change of price movements. When wielded skillfully, it can offer day traders a distinct advantage in identifying market trends, reversals, and potential entry or exit points with a high degree of accuracy.

This book is not just about introducing you to RSI as another indicator; it's about transforming your trading approach and elevating your results.

Why RSI Matters in Short-Term Trading

When engaging in day trading, every tick of the market matters. Prices can change in seconds, and fortunes can be made—or lost—at a moment's notice. For day traders,

8

navigating this dynamic landscape requires a robust and reliable toolset. This is where RSI makes its impact felt.

RSI is a momentum oscillator that ranges from 0 to 100, offering traders insights into whether an asset is overbought or oversold. Unlike more complex indicators that may present conflicting data, RSI distills essential market information into a straightforward signal. When used correctly, it allows traders to anticipate potential reversals, confirm trends, and make confident decisions about when to enter or exit trades.

In short-term trading, timing is everything. With its ability to highlight shifts in momentum, RSI provides a crucial edge. By analyzing price movement strength and identifying market exhaustion, traders can make better-informed decisions, mitigate risks, and capitalize on fleeting opportunities.

Understanding why RSI matters is the first step in mastering its use. Through this book, you will learn not only how to interpret RSI readings but also how to integrate it seamlessly with other tools, adapt it to your preferred trading style, and refine it for specific market conditions. Ultimately, my aim is to make RSI an indispensable part of your day trading arsenal.

Goals and Objectives of This Book

The overarching goal of this book is simple yet profound: to help you become a successful day trader by mastering the use of the Relative Strength Index. This book is designed to take you on a journey from understanding the fundamentals of RSI to employing advanced strategies that yield consistent results.

Here are the key objectives we'll achieve together:

Comprehensive Understanding: You will gain a thorough understanding of what RSI is, how it works, and how to apply it effectively in different market conditions.

Practical Strategies: We will explore proven RSI-based strategies tailored specifically for day trading, equipping you with practical tools to achieve consistent gains.

Risk Management Techniques: Successful trading requires managing risk. This book will guide you on using RSI not just to identify trades but also to protect your capital.

Real-World Applications: Learning from theory is important, but applying it is critical. Real-world examples and case studies will illustrate how to use RSI in various market scenarios.

By the end of this book, you will be equipped with both the knowledge and confidence to integrate RSI into your day trading strategy and make smarter, data-driven decisions.

How to Use This Book Effectively

This book has been structured to maximize your learning and success with the Relative Strength Index. It is divided into clear, progressive chapters, each building on the knowledge and skills introduced earlier. For optimal results, we recommend that you approach this book as a practical guide rather than a theoretical textbook.

Begin with the basics, even if you are familiar with RSI. Revisiting core principles can offer new insights and set a solid foundation for more advanced techniques. As you progress, I encourage you to take notes, reflect on examples, and, where applicable, practice the strategies in a demo trading environment before implementing them with real funds.

Throughout the chapters, you will find practical exercises and checkpoints to test your understanding and reinforce key concepts. Make use of these resources. Engage actively, and don't be afraid to revisit sections or seek clarification on complex ideas. Trading success is not achieved overnight—it's built through dedication, learning, and hands-on experience.

Above all, remember that this book is a guide tailored to your growth as a trader. Keep an open mind, stay disciplined, and never stop learning. The market rewards those who adapt, learn, and execute with precision.

Avery Welles

Chapter 1

Foundations of the Relative Strength Index (RSI)

The Relative Strength Index (RSI), Created by J. Welles Wilder Jr., an engineer turned technical analyst, the RSI was first introduced to the trading community in his 1978 book, 'New Concepts in Technical Trading Systems'. This seminal work laid the groundwork for many modern trading strategies and indicators, but it was the RSI that captured the attention of traders for its intuitive approach to measuring market momentum.

Wilder's motivation for developing the RSI stemmed from a desire to create a straightforward, easy-to-use tool that could assess the speed and change of price movements over a specified period. Unlike other complex indicators that required extensive computation, RSI was designed to be accessible and actionable, even to traders without a deep background in mathematics. Its primary purpose was to help traders identify potential reversal points in the market by measuring whether a particular asset was overbought or oversold.

The RSI accomplishes this by oscillating between 0 and 100, with values above 70 traditionally indicating that an asset may be overbought and values below 30 suggesting that it may be oversold. This simplified range allowed traders to quickly gauge market sentiment and make informed decisions about entering or exiting trades.

Over the years, Wilder's creation has remained a mainstay in the trading world, valued for its versatility, adaptability, and ability to work across different asset classes and timeframes. Today, the RSI is used by traders of all experience levels, from retail investors to institutional players. It has proven its worth not only as a tool for identifying potential turning points in the market but also as a means of confirming trends, analyzing momentum, and managing risk.

Basic RSI Calculation

At its core, the Relative Strength Index is a momentum oscillator that compares the magnitude of recent gains to recent losses over a specific period, typically 14 periods. While this may sound complex, the calculation itself is relatively straightforward and can be broken down into a few key steps:

1. Calculating Average Gains and Losses:

To determine the RSI, the first step is to calculate the average gain and average loss over the chosen period. For example, if you are using a 14-period RSI, you would calculate the average gain and average loss over the past 14 periods (e.g., 14 days for daily charts).

- Average Gain = Sum of Gains over the past 14 periods / 14
- Average Loss = Sum of Losses over the past 14 periods / 14

2. Calculating the Relative Strength (RS):

The next step involves dividing the average gain by the average loss to obtain the Relative Strength (RS).

RS = Average Gain / Average Loss

3. Calculating the RSI Value:

Finally, the RSI is derived using the following formula:

RSI = 100 - [100 / (1 + RS)]

The resulting value will range between 0 and 100. As mentioned earlier, RSI readings above 70 are generally considered to indicate overbought conditions, while

Avery Welles

readings below 30 suggest oversold conditions. These levels
can, however, be adjusted based on market context, trader
preferences, or specific strategies.

Example Calculation:

Suppose a stock has experienced the following gains and
losses over the past 14 days:

- Total Gains: 20 points
- Total Losses: 10 points
- Average Gain = 20 / 14 = 1.43
- Average Loss = 10 / 14 = 0.71
- RS = 1.43 / 0.71 ≈ 2.01
- RSI = 100 - [100 / (1 + 2.01)] ≈ 66.67

In this example, the RSI value of approximately 66.67
indicates that the stock is nearing overbought territory but
has not yet crossed the critical threshold of 70. Traders
could interpret this as a signal to monitor the asset closely

for signs of a potential reversal or continued upward momentum.

Practical Use in Trading:

The simplicity of the RSI calculation belies its practical utility. By condensing market movement data into a single, interpretable figure, RSI allows traders to quickly assess market conditions and make informed decisions. It works across different timeframes—daily, hourly, or even minute charts—and can be adapted to various trading styles, including swing trading, scalping, and position trading.

For day traders, RSI's ability to identify short-term overbought and oversold conditions can be particularly useful. By combining RSI readings with other technical indicators and chart patterns, traders can develop robust strategies that take advantage of momentum shifts and market reversals. As we continue through this book, we will explore these strategies in greater depth, but first, let's compare RSI with other popular technical indicators.

RSI vs. Other Technical Indicators

The Relative Strength Index is often compared to other popular technical indicators, such as Moving Averages, Moving Average Convergence Divergence (MACD), and Stochastic Oscillators. While each of these tools has its unique strengths, understanding how RSI differs from—and complements—these indicators can enhance a trader's ability to analyze the market.

RSI vs. Moving Averages:

Moving averages are widely used to smooth out price data and identify trends. The Simple Moving Average (SMA) and the Exponential Moving Average (EMA) are the most common types. Moving averages help traders determine the overall direction of the market and provide signals when prices cross above or below these averages.

However, they lag behind current price movements due to their reliance on historical data.

RSI, on the other hand, provides a more immediate view of market momentum and conditions. While moving averages are useful for trend-following, RSI excels in identifying potential reversal points, allowing traders to anticipate changes in market direction rather than react to them. Many traders use RSI and moving averages together, relying on RSI for momentum analysis and moving averages for trend confirmation.

RSI vs. MACD:

The MACD is another popular momentum indicator that uses two moving averages of different periods to identify changes in trend strength, direction, and duration. Unlike RSI, which is bounded between 0 and 100, MACD is unbounded, which means it does not have predefined overbought or oversold levels.

MACD signals are typically generated when the MACD line crosses above or below its signal line or when the MACD histogram shifts.

The key difference between MACD and RSI lies in their focus. While MACD measures the relationship between two moving averages, RSI focuses on the magnitude of price changes over a specified period. As a result, RSI is often seen as more sensitive to short-term price movements, making it ideal for identifying overbought or oversold conditions in shorter timeframes. Traders often use MACD and RSI together to gain a more comprehensive view of market momentum and potential turning points.

RSI vs. Stochastic Oscillator:

The Stochastic Oscillator, like RSI, is a momentum indicator that oscillates between 0 and 100. It compares a security's closing price to its price range over a specified period, providing a measure of momentum. The main difference between the two indicators is the way they

_ Welles*

measure momentum. While RSI measures price changes relative to recent gains and losses, the Stochastic Oscillator measures the position of the closing price relative to the high-low range over a given period.

Traders often use both RSI and the Stochastic Oscillator in tandem to confirm signals. For example, if both indicators show that an asset is overbought, it strengthens the case for a potential reversal. Conversely, if one indicator shows overbought conditions while the other does not, it may signal caution or indicate that further confirmation is needed before taking action.

RSI's Unique Value:

What sets RSI apart from many other indicators is its versatility and simplicity. Unlike more complex tools, RSI provides actionable insights with minimal input and can be adapted to a wide range of trading strategies. Its ability to highlight overbought and oversold conditions, combined

Copyrighted Materials **24**

with its straightforward calculation, makes it an accessible yet powerful tool for traders of all levels.

Common Myths and Misconceptions about RSI

Despite its widespread use and proven effectiveness, several myths and misconceptions about RSI persist within the trading community. Dispelling these myths is crucial for traders to fully leverage the power of this indicator.

Myth 1: RSI Always Signals a Reversal at 70/30 Levels

One of the most common misconceptions is that RSI values above 70 or below 30 always signal an imminent market reversal. While RSI levels above 70 may indicate that an asset is overbought and levels below 30 suggest it is oversold, these thresholds do not guarantee a reversal. Markets can remain in overbought or oversold conditions for extended periods, especially during strong trends.

Instead of treating the 70/30 levels as hard triggers for entering or exiting trades, savvy traders use them as cautionary flags. They may wait for confirmation from other indicators or look for signs of divergence between RSI and price action before making a decision.

Myth 2: RSI Is Ineffective in Trending Markets

Another misconception is that RSI is only useful in range-bound markets and loses its effectiveness during strong trends. While it is true that RSI often performs well in sideways markets, it can still be valuable in trending markets when used correctly. By adjusting the overbought and oversold levels (e.g., 80/20 instead of 70/30) or combining RSI with trend-following indicators, traders can better adapt their strategies to different market conditions.

Myth 3: RSI Settings Should Never Be Changed

The default RSI period of 14 is widely used, but it is not a one-size-fits-all solution. Different market conditions, timeframes, and trading styles may require adjustments to the RSI settings. Shortening the period (e.g., to 7 or 9) can make RSI more sensitive, while lengthening it (e.g., to 20 or 25) can smooth out its signals. The key is to test and adapt the settings to align with your specific trading goals and preferences.

Myth 4: RSI Is a Standalone Indicator

Some traders mistakenly believe that RSI can be used in isolation to consistently predict market movements. While RSI is a powerful tool, it is most effective when used in conjunction with other indicators, chart patterns, and market analysis techniques. By combining RSI with other tools—such as moving averages, support and resistance levels, or volume analysis—traders can increase their chances of success and reduce the likelihood of false signals.

Myth 5: RSI Has No Place in Long-Term Trading

Although RSI is commonly associated with short-term trading strategies, it can also be applied to longer-term trading and investing. By adjusting the RSI period and using weekly or monthly charts, traders and investors can gain insights into long-term market trends, identify cyclical patterns, and make strategic decisions.

Overall, by using RSI with a clear understanding of its strengths, limitations, and nuances, you can harness its full potential and avoid common pitfalls that often lead to suboptimal trading outcomes.

Chapter 2

Essential Principles of Day Trading

A trader's mindset can often make the difference between consistent success and a string of costly losses. While technical knowledge, market insights, and strategies are all critical components of day trading, the psychological aspect plays an equally pivotal role. To succeed as a day trader, one must master not only market analysis but also the art of self-discipline, emotional control, and strategic thinking.

Day trading is inherently volatile. The markets can move rapidly, and prices may shift dramatically within minutes or even seconds. This environment naturally gives rise to a roller coaster of emotions—excitement, fear, greed, anxiety, and frustration—all of which can cloud judgment and lead to impulsive decisions. For example, when a trade goes well and produces a profit, the rush of euphoria can lead traders to become overconfident, taking excessive risks without fully assessing potential downsides. Conversely, a sudden loss may trigger panic, causing traders to exit positions prematurely or "revenge trade" in an attempt to recover their losses quickly.

The key to managing these emotions lies in cultivating a balanced, disciplined mindset. Successful day traders learn to detach themselves emotionally from individual trades, viewing each one as part of a larger strategy. They accept losses as part of the trading process and do not let fear or frustration dictate their next move. Equally, they do not allow winning trades to lead to recklessness or overconfidence. By maintaining emotional equilibrium, traders can approach each trade with a clear, objective mindset and execute their strategies with precision.

Winning Strategies for Day Trading Psychology

1. Develop and Follow a Trading Plan:

A solid trading plan serves as a roadmap, outlining entry and exit points, stop-loss levels, risk management guidelines, and overall trading goals. Sticking to this plan helps traders avoid impulsive decisions driven by market noise or emotional reactions.

2. Set Realistic Expectations:

Day trading is not a guaranteed path to instant wealth. Many beginners fall into the trap of expecting huge profits from every trade, only to be disappointed by market fluctuations.

Successful traders understand that losses are inevitable and focus on achieving consistent, incremental gains over time.

3. Embrace Risk Management:

Protecting capital is the top priority in day trading. This means setting stop-loss orders to limit potential losses, managing position sizes based on risk tolerance, and never risking more than a small percentage of one's total capital on a single trade. Proper risk management reduces the psychological impact of losses and ensures that no single trade can wipe out a trading account.

4. Cultivate Patience and Discipline:

Not every market move presents a profitable trading opportunity. Winning traders know when to wait on the sidelines, avoiding trades that do not meet their criteria. Patience prevents overtrading, while discipline ensures that trades align with a well-defined strategy.

5. Maintain a Positive Mindset:

A resilient mindset is crucial for navigating the ups and downs of day trading. Successful traders learn from their mistakes, adapt to changing market conditions, and approach each day as a fresh opportunity to improve their skills and strategies.

Common Losing Strategies and Psychological Pitfalls

1. Overtrading:

Driven by impatience or the desire to recoup losses quickly, some traders engage in excessive trading, often entering positions without a clear plan.

Overtrading can lead to poor decision-making, higher transaction costs, and increased risk.

2. FOMO (Fear of Missing Out):

The fear of missing out on a potential profit can lead traders to chase market moves that are already underway, often resulting in poor entry points and unfavorable risk-to-reward ratios. Effective traders wait for their setups and do not let FOMO dictate their trades.

3. Ignoring Risk Management:

Failing to set stop-loss orders or risking too much capital on a single trade can lead to catastrophic losses. Even experienced traders can fall victim to this mistake if they become overconfident or let emotions take over.

4. Revenge Trading:

After experiencing a loss, some traders attempt to "get back" at the market by taking aggressive, impulsive trades in an attempt to recover their losses quickly. This often leads to further losses and emotional turmoil.

5. Inability to Adapt:

Markets are constantly changing, and what worked yesterday may not work today. Rigidly sticking to a strategy without adapting to new conditions can lead to poor performance over time.

By mastering the psychological aspects of day trading and avoiding common pitfalls, traders can improve their decision-making, reduce stress, and increase their chances of long-term success.

Market Analysis for Day Traders

Unlike long-term investors who focus on macroeconomic factors and fundamental analysis, day traders must analyze the market on shorter timeframes, often making rapid decisions based on price movements, volume, and technical indicators.

Technical vs. Fundamental Analysis

While both forms of analysis have their merits, day traders tend to rely more heavily on technical analysis. This approach focuses on analyzing historical price and volume data to predict future market movements. Common tools used in technical analysis include chart patterns, candlestick formations, support and resistance levels, moving averages, and oscillators like the RSI (Relative Strength Index), MACD, and Stochastic Oscillator.

Fundamental analysis, which involves evaluating a company's financial health, industry trends, economic conditions, and news events, plays a less prominent role in day trading.

However, day traders may still pay attention to key economic releases (e.g., employment reports, interest rate decisions) or major news events that can cause sudden volatility in the market.

Key Aspects of Market Analysis for Day Traders

1. Trend Identification:

Determining whether the market is in an uptrend, downtrend, or ranging is crucial for selecting the right trading strategy. Trend-following traders look for opportunities to ride market momentum, while range traders focus on buying low and selling high within established price boundaries.

2. Support and Resistance Levels:

Support levels represent price points where buying interest is strong enough to prevent further declines, while resistance levels act as barriers to upward movement. Identifying these levels helps traders determine entry and exit points, as well as areas where price reversals may occur.

3. Candlestick Patterns and Chart Patterns:

Candlestick patterns, such as doji, engulfing patterns, and hammers, provide insights into market sentiment and potential reversals. Chart patterns, including head and shoulders, double tops/bottoms, and triangles, can signal trend continuation or reversal.

4. Volume Analysis:

Volume measures the number of shares or contracts traded within a given period. High volume often confirms the strength of a price move, while low volume may indicate a lack of conviction. Volume spikes can signal breakouts, reversals, or heightened market interest.

5. Market Sentiment Indicators:

Sentiment indicators gauge the overall mood of market participants. Tools like the VIX (Volatility Index) or put-call ratios can provide insights into market fear, complacency, or optimism. Day traders may use sentiment data to anticipate market turning points or gauge the strength of trends.

6. Timeframes:

Day traders analyze markets on shorter timeframes, such as 1-minute, 5-minute, or 15-minute charts. Each timeframe offers different levels of detail, with lower timeframes providing rapid signals and higher timeframes offering broader context. Traders often use multiple timeframes to gain a comprehensive view of market dynamics.

Building a Day Trading Strategy Based on Market Analysis
To succeed in day trading, it is essential to develop a strategy based on thorough market analysis. This strategy should outline entry and exit criteria, risk management rules, and conditions for trade setup validation.

Key Tools and Platforms for Trading Success

The modern day trader has access to a wide range of tools, platforms, and technologies designed to enhance trading performance.

Trading Platforms

A robust trading platform is a trader's central hub for executing trades, analyzing market data, and managing their account. Key features to look for in a trading platform include:

1. Real-Time Data and Charting:

Accurate, real-time market data and advanced charting capabilities are essential for day trading. Platforms should offer a variety of chart types, technical indicators, drawing tools, and customizable settings to support detailed market analysis.

2. Order Execution Speed:

In the fast-paced world of day trading, execution speed is critical. Delays in order execution can result in missed opportunities or suboptimal entry and exit points. High-quality platforms prioritize fast, reliable order processing to minimize slippage.

3. User-Friendly Interface:

An intuitive, easy-to-navigate interface allows traders to quickly access market data, execute trades, and monitor open positions. Complex or cluttered interfaces can lead to errors or slower decision-making.

4. Risk Management Tools:

Platforms that offer built-in risk management features, such as stop-loss orders, take-profit orders, and position sizing calculators, enable traders to protect their capital and control risk on each trade.

5. Customizable Alerts:

Alerts based on price levels, technical indicators, or other criteria help traders stay informed about market movements and potential trade setups.

Tools for Market Analysis

In addition to trading platforms, day traders rely on a variety of tools to analyze market conditions and develop strategies:

1. Charting Software:

Advanced charting software provides comprehensive tools for technical analysis, including customizable indicators, multi-timeframe views, and pattern recognition capabilities.

2. News Feeds and Economic Calendars:

Staying informed about news events and economic releases that may impact the market is critical for day traders. Real-time news feeds and economic calendars help traders anticipate volatility and plan accordingly.

3. Screening Tools:

Stock, forex, or crypto screeners allow traders to filter assets based on specific criteria, such as volume, price changes, or technical patterns. This helps identify potential trading opportunities quickly.

RSI Divergences

RSI divergences occur when the price of an asset moves in the opposite direction of the RSI. For example, if the price makes a new high while the RSI makes a lower high, it indicates a bearish divergence, which may signal a potential trend reversal. Conversely, if the price makes a new low

Avery Welles

while the RSI makes a higher low, it indicates a bullish divergence, suggesting a possible upward reversal. Identifying and trading divergences can provide valuable signals for day traders.

Chapter 3

Advanced Techniques for Consistent Gains

The RSI Range Strategy: Trading Ranges and Volatile Markets

One advanced approach for using the Relative Strength Index (RSI) involves trading within market ranges and during periods of heightened volatility. The RSI Range Strategy is designed to exploit price oscillations within a specified boundary and take advantage of the frequent reversals that occur in such environments. Unlike trend-following strategies that aim to capture directional moves, range trading seeks to profit from buying low (support levels) and selling high (resistance levels) or vice versa.

Identifying Market Ranges

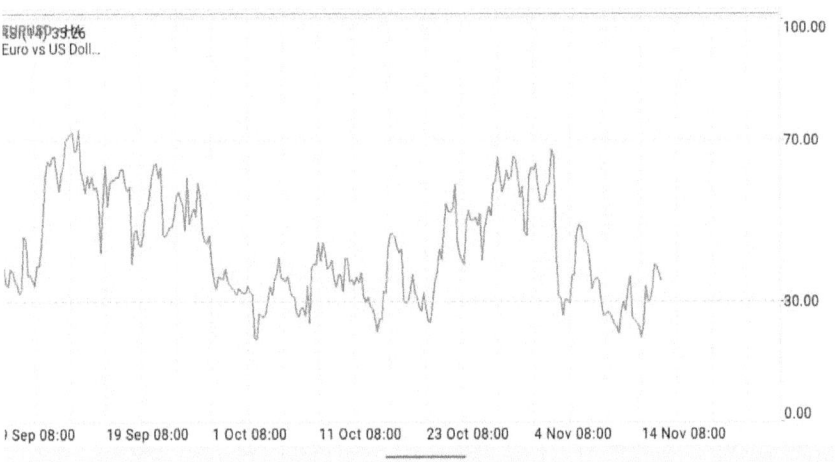

Before implementing the RSI Range Strategy, it's crucial to identify when the market is in a range-bound state. Unlike trending markets characterized by higher highs and higher lows (uptrend) or lower highs and lower lows (downtrend), range-bound markets fluctuate between established support and resistance levels. These levels often act as psychological barriers where buyers and sellers interact, causing the price to oscillate within a confined zone.

To identify market ranges:

- **Visual Analysis**: Examine historical price movements on the chart to identify areas where the price consistently moves between a horizontal support and resistance band.

- **Bollinger Bands**: This indicator can help traders identify when the market is consolidating, as price tends to move within the upper and lower bands during range-bound phases.

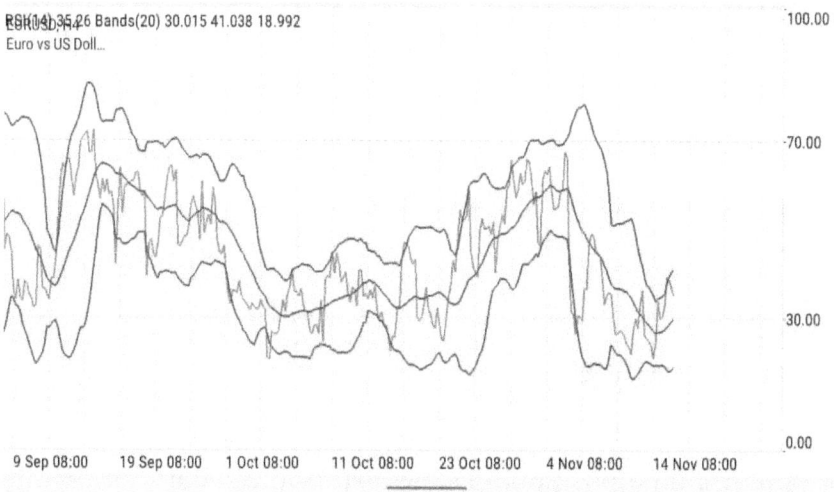

- **Average True Range (ATR):** Declining ATR values indicate a reduction in volatility, suggesting a range-bound market.

Applying the RSI Range Strategy

Once a range has been identified, the RSI can be used to pinpoint optimal entry and exit points. The traditional overbought (70) and oversold (30) levels on the RSI scale often work well in range-bound markets but can be fine-tuned based on specific conditions or historical performance of the asset.

1. Buy Setup:

- Wait for the RSI to move below 30, signaling that the asset may be oversold and due for a rebound.

- Confirm that the price is near or at the established support level of the range.

- Enter a long position, placing a stop-loss slightly below the support level to minimize risk.

2. Sell Setup:

- Wait for the RSI to move above 70, indicating that the asset may be overbought and due for a correction.

- Confirm that the price is near or at the established resistance level of the range.

- Enter a short position, placing a stop-loss slightly above the resistance level.

Managing Volatility and Breakouts

One potential challenge with the RSI Range Strategy is dealing with breakouts—when the price moves beyond the established range, leading to a new trend. Breakouts can result in significant losses if traders are caught on the wrong side of the market. To mitigate this risk:

- Use Trailing Stops: A trailing stop can lock in profits as the price moves favorably, while also protecting against a reversal.

- Be Prepared to Reverse: If a breakout occurs with strong momentum, consider reversing your position to align with the new trend. Confirmation tools, such as volume spikes or candlestick patterns, can help verify the validity of the breakout.

The RSI Range Strategy works best in stable, range-bound markets and should be avoided in strong trending environments unless modified with additional tools for trend identification.

Using RSI with Moving Averages, MACD, and Other Indicators

Each indicator offers unique insights into market conditions, and integrating them allows traders to build a more comprehensive trading strategy.

RSI and Moving Averages

Moving averages are one of the simplest yet most effective tools for identifying trends. Combining RSI with moving averages can help filter out false signals and confirm the direction of the market trend.

- **Trend Confirmation:** When the RSI indicates an overbought or oversold condition, use a moving average (e.g., 50-day or 200-day simple moving average) to determine whether the broader market trend aligns with the signal. For example, if the RSI indicates that the asset is oversold, a buy signal is more credible if the price is trading above the long-term moving average (indicating an uptrend).

- **Crossovers:** Short-term and long-term moving average crossovers can act as confirmation signals for RSI-based trades. For example, if a short-term moving average crosses above a long-term moving average (bullish crossover) while the RSI is moving out of oversold territory, it strengthens the case for a long position.

RSI and MACD (Moving Average Convergence Divergence)

The MACD is a momentum indicator that compares two moving averages of an asset's price and plots the difference as a histogram, along with a signal line. Combining RSI with MACD allows traders to cross-verify momentum shifts and potential reversals.

- **Double Confirmation:** When the RSI shows overbought or oversold conditions, look for confirmation from the MACD histogram crossing the zero line or the MACD line crossing above/below the signal line. This double confirmation increases the likelihood of a successful trade.

- **Divergences:** Both RSI and MACD can identify divergences between price movement and indicator signals. When both indicators show divergences (e.g., price makes a higher high, but both RSI and MACD make lower highs), it strongly signals a potential trend reversal.

Combining RSI with Other Indicators

- **Stochastic Oscillator:** Both RSI and the stochastic oscillator measure momentum, but they use different calculations. Combining them can provide additional confirmation of overbought and oversold conditions.

- **Bollinger Bands:** Bollinger Bands measure volatility and can provide context for RSI signals. When the RSI indicates an oversold condition and the price touches the lower Bollinger Band, it may present a strong buy opportunity.

- **Volume Indicators:** Volume-based indicators, such as On-Balance Volume (OBV) or the Accumulation/Distribution Line, provide insights into the strength of a price move. RSI signals supported by strong volume are more reliable than those occurring on low volume.

By combining RSI with complementary indicators, traders can reduce the likelihood of false signals, improve their entry and exit timing, and better manage risk.

Fine-Tuning RSI Parameters for Greater Accuracy

The default RSI setting of a 14-period lookback is widely used, but it is not always the optimal choice for every market condition or trading style. Fine-tuning RSI parameters involves adjusting the period length and overbought/oversold levels to better suit your trading strategy.

Adjusting the RSI Period

- Shorter Periods (e.g., 7 or 9): Shortening the RSI period makes it more sensitive to recent price movements, generating more frequent signals. This can be beneficial for day traders who need quick entries and exits but may also result in more false signals.

- Longer Periods (e.g., 20 or 25): Lengthening the RSI period smooths out its movements and reduces the frequency of signals. This approach is useful for capturing more significant trends and reducing noise, but it may lead to delayed entry and exit points.

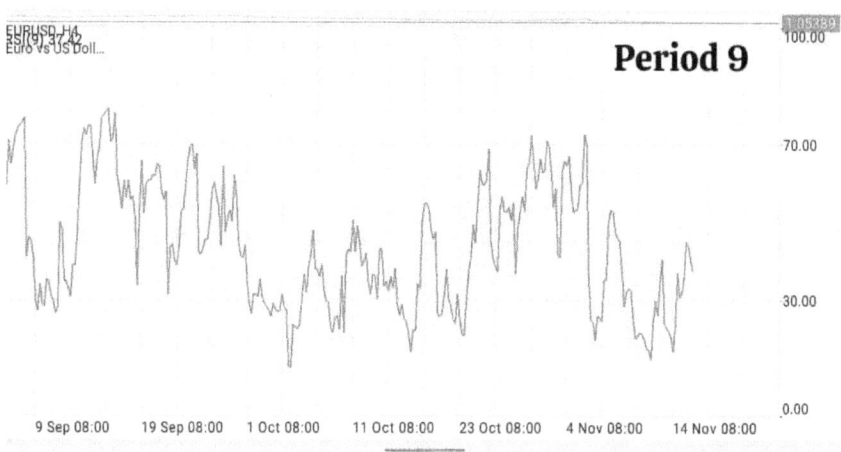

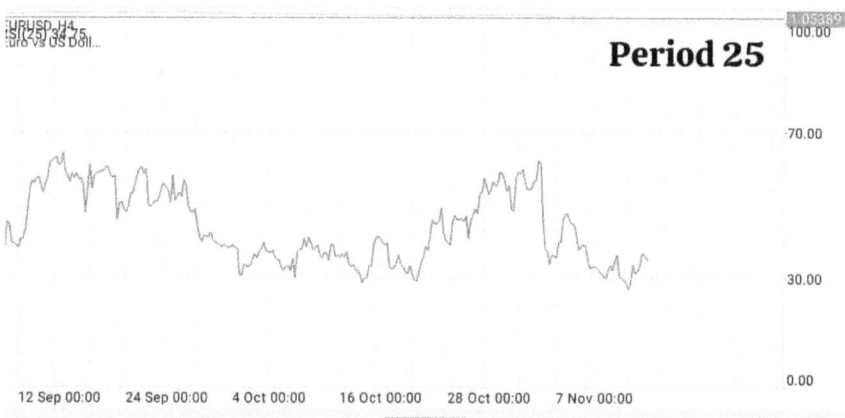

Customizing Overbought/Oversold Levels

The traditional levels of 70 (overbought) and 30 (oversold) are effective for many scenarios but may not work optimally in all markets.

- **Tighter Levels (e.g., 80/20):** Raising the overbought level to 80 and lowering the oversold level to 20 can reduce the frequency of signals, making them more reliable but less frequent. This adjustment is useful for strong trending markets where prices can remain in overbought/oversold zones for extended periods.

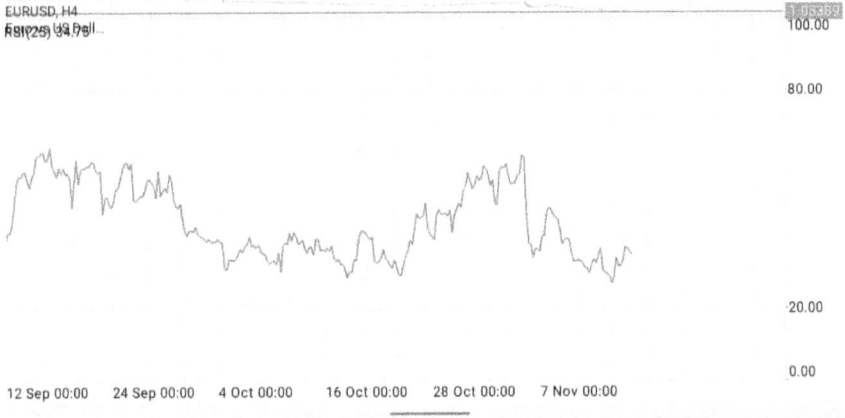

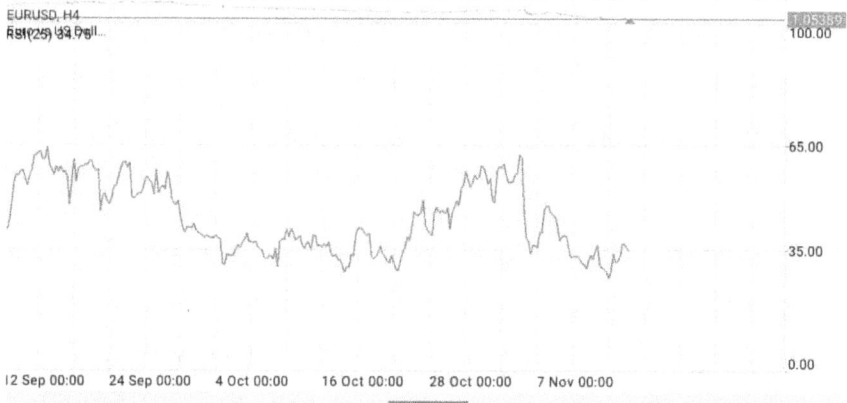

- Looser Levels (e.g., 65/35): Lowering the overbought threshold to 65 and raising the oversold threshold to 35 can increase the frequency of signals, which may be beneficial for highly volatile markets.

Optimizing RSI for Specific Markets

Different markets exhibit unique characteristics and volatility profiles. For example:

- Equity Markets: Stock prices often exhibit strong trends and sudden reversals, making a shorter RSI period (e.g., 9) effective for capturing rapid moves.

- Forex Markets: Currency pairs tend to experience prolonged trends, so using a longer RSI period (e.g., 21) may provide more reliable signals.

- Crypto Markets: Cryptocurrencies are known for high volatility, making customized overbought/oversold levels and adaptive RSI periods valuable for managing risk.

Testing different RSI configurations on historical data (backtesting) helps identify settings that align with your preferred market and trading style. Fine-tuning the RSI to your specific needs can enhance the accuracy of your signals and improve overall trading performance.

Multi-Timeframe Analysis: Maximizing Trade Potential

Multi-timeframe analysis (MTA) involves examining the same asset on different timeframes to gain a broader perspective on market trends and identify high-probability trade setups. Integrating RSI into a multi-timeframe approach allows traders to align their short-term trades with the overall market context, improving the consistency of gains.

Markets often exhibit different behaviors on various timeframes. For example, an asset may be in a strong uptrend on a daily chart but experiencing a minor correction on an hourly chart. By analyzing multiple timeframes, traders can identify the dominant trend, avoid counter-trend trades, and spot potential reversal points with greater accuracy.

Using RSI Across Multiple Timeframes

To apply RSI in a multi-timeframe approach:

1. Identify the Dominant Trend:

Start by analyzing a higher timeframe (e.g., daily or 4-hour chart) to determine the overall market trend. Use RSI to confirm whether the market is overbought, oversold, or trending steadily.

2. Find Entry Points on Lower Timeframes:

Once the dominant trend is established, switch to a lower timeframe (e.g., 1-hour or 15-minute chart) to identify precise entry and exit points. For example, if the higher timeframe RSI indicates a bullish trend, look for oversold signals on the lower timeframe RSI to enter a long position.

Combining RSI Signals Across Timeframes

- Trend Continuation Trades: If the RSI on a higher timeframe indicates an uptrend and the lower timeframe RSI becomes oversold, this may present a high-probability opportunity to enter a long position in line with the dominant trend.

- Reversal Trades: If the RSI on a higher timeframe shows overbought conditions and begins to diverge, it may signal an impending reversal. Use the lower timeframe to confirm the reversal before entering a counter-trend trade.

Multi-timeframe analysis helps filter out false signals that might appear on a single timeframe. By confirming signals across multiple timeframes, traders gain a more comprehensive understanding of market dynamics and reduce the likelihood of making impulsive trades too.

Avery Welles

Chapter 5

Risk Management in Day Trading with RSI

Day trading offers a fast-paced and potentially lucrative way to profit from financial markets. However, it also comes with substantial risk, particularly when using technical indicators like the Relative Strength Index (RSI). Effective risk management is the foundation on which consistent profitability is built.

Position Sizing and Risk-Reward Ratios

One of the core elements of risk management in day trading is position sizing—deciding how much capital to allocate to each trade. Incorrectly sizing a position can lead to excessive losses or missed opportunities, while proper position sizing maximizes profitability while keeping risk at an acceptable level.

The Importance of Position Sizing

Position sizing determines how much you are willing to risk on a particular trade. By controlling the size of your trades relative to your total capital, you can withstand inevitable losses and continue to trade with confidence. Even highly skilled traders experience losing streaks, but those with effective risk management strategies emerge from them intact.

Determining Position Size

A common approach to position sizing is to risk a fixed percentage of your trading capital on any single trade, typically ranging from 1% to 3%. The calculation for determining position size is straightforward:

Position Size = Account Risk \ Trade Risk (Difference between Entry and Stop-Loss Price)

For example, if your account balance is $10,000 and you are willing to risk 2% per trade, your maximum account risk is $200. If you enter a trade at $50 per share with a stop-loss at $45 (a $5 risk per share), you can buy up to 40 shares ($200 ÷ $5).

Risk-Reward Ratios

The risk-reward ratio is another critical aspect of managing trades effectively. This ratio compares the potential profit of a trade to its potential loss. A risk-reward ratio of 1:2, for instance, means that for every dollar risked, the expected gain is two dollars. Higher ratios are preferred, as they allow traders to be wrong more often while still maintaining profitability.

Copyrighted Materials   **65**

Recommendations for Position Sizing and Risk-Reward Management

- Stick to a Consistent Risk Per Trade: Maintain a fixed percentage of your account balance as risk per trade. This prevents emotional decision-making and keeps you disciplined during both winning and losing streaks.

- Aim for Favorable Risk-Reward Ratios: Enter trades with at least a 1:2 or 1:3 risk-reward ratio to ensure that profitable trades outweigh losing ones.

- Adjust Size Based on Market Conditions: In volatile markets, reduce position sizes to minimize risk. Conversely, in stable markets, you may consider slightly increasing your risk allocation when conditions align with your strategy.

Stop-Loss Strategies for Protecting Your Trades

Stop-loss orders are a fundamental tool in risk management. They define the maximum loss you are willing to accept on a trade, allowing you to exit positions automatically when the market moves against you. Without effective stop-loss strategies, even a few losing trades can erode your trading capital.

Types of Stop-Loss Orders

1. Fixed Stop-Loss: This is a predetermined price level set below (or above, for short positions) your entry point. It ensures that your loss is limited to a specific amount.

2. Trailing Stop-Loss: This type of stop-loss follows the price as it moves in your favor but remains fixed when the price moves against you. Trailing stops are useful for locking in profits while allowing for continued upside potential.

3. Volatility-Based Stop-Loss: This approach adjusts the stop-loss based on market volatility. For example, if the market is highly volatile, the stop-loss is placed further away from the entry point to avoid being prematurely triggered by market noise.

Setting Stop-Loss Levels with RSI

When trading with the RSI, stop-loss orders can be strategically placed based on RSI levels and price structure:

- RSI Overbought/Oversold Zones: If entering a trade based on RSI overbought or oversold signals, place the stop-loss just beyond the recent high (for short positions) or low (for long positions).

- RSI Divergences: When trading based on RSI divergences, the stop-loss can be set at the point where the divergence is invalidated.

Recommendations for Stop-Loss Placement

1. Use Multiple Stop-Loss Techniques: Combining different stop-loss methods, such as fixed and trailing stops, can provide flexibility and enhanced protection.

2. Account for Market Conditions: Adapt your stop-loss strategy based on market volatility and liquidity. Tight stops are suitable for stable markets, while wider stops may be necessary in highly volatile conditions.

3. Respect Your Stop-Loss: Never move or remove a stop-loss to "give the trade more room" without a well-defined rationale. Doing so can lead to large, unintended losses.

Managing Leverage and Margin Effectively

Leverage allows traders to control larger positions with a relatively small amount of capital, magnifying both potential gains and potential losses. Margin trading involves borrowing funds to increase the size of a position. While leverage and margin can increase profitability, they also carry substantial risk.

Leverage is a double-edged sword. While it can amplify returns, it also magnifies losses. Traders who do not manage leverage effectively may face margin calls—

demands from their broker to deposit more funds to cover losses—or even lose their entire account balance.

Margin Requirements and Maintenance

Brokers typically set margin requirements, which represent the minimum account balance you must maintain to keep your leveraged positions open. Falling below this level triggers a margin call, which can lead to forced liquidation of your positions.

Best Practices for Managing Leverage

1. Use Leverage Prudently: Only use leverage when you have a well-defined trading strategy with strict risk controls. High leverage is unnecessary for most day trading strategies and often leads to emotional decision-making.

2. Set Realistic Leverage Limits: Establish a maximum leverage limit for your trades, and stick to it. Lower leverage reduces risk exposure and makes it easier to withstand market fluctuations.

3. Monitor Margin Levels Closely: Regularly monitor your margin levels to avoid margin calls. Keeping a buffer of unused margin can provide flexibility during periods of high market volatility.

Psychological Challenges of Risk Management

The human element is often the most challenging aspect of risk management in day trading. Even with well-defined rules and strategies, emotions like fear, greed, and frustration can lead to impulsive decisions that undermine your trading plan.

1. Overcoming Fear and Anxiety: Fear can prevent traders from executing trades or cause them to exit positions prematurely. This often occurs after a string of losses or when entering a large position. To combat fear:

- Focus on the Process: Shift your mindset from profit-and-loss outcomes to executing your strategy with discipline. Trust in your risk management rules and the probabilities they imply.

- Reduce Position Sizes: If fear is overwhelming, temporarily trade smaller positions until confidence is restored.

2. Controlling Greed: Greed leads traders to take excessive risks, such as overleveraging, holding onto winning trades for too long, or abandoning stop-loss orders in pursuit of unrealistic gains. To manage greed:

- Set Realistic Goals: Establish daily or weekly profit targets, and be willing to walk away from the market once those goals are achieved.

- Stick to Your Plan: Do not deviate from your predefined risk management rules, even if the market appears to be offering "easy" opportunities.

3. Handling Losses: Losses are an inevitable part of trading. However, how you respond to them determines your long-term success. It is crucial to:

- Avoid Revenge Trading: Trying to recover losses quickly by entering impulsive trades often leads to greater losses.

- Review Your Trades: Analyze losing trades to identify mistakes and learn from them. Continuous improvement is essential for consistent success.

Overall, all this will not only protect your trading capital but also create the conditions necessary for long-term success using the RSI and other technical indicators.

Avery Welles

74

Chapter 6

Automated Trading Systems with RSI

Automation in trading is no longer a niche reserved for institutional traders and tech-savvy retail investors. As markets grow increasingly complex and fast-paced, day traders are turning to automated systems to gain a competitive edge. At the core of these systems lies a simple truth: algorithms can process vast amounts of data with speed and precision that no human can match.

For traders using the Relative Strength Index (RSI), automated strategies present a powerful opportunity to amplify their edge while minimizing emotional decision-making.

Developing and Testing RSI-Based Algorithms

Creating a successful automated trading system begins with translating your RSI-based strategy into a set of rules that a computer can execute. This requires a clear understanding of how RSI works, the logic behind your trading decisions, and the necessary parameters for automation.

Step 1: Define Your Trading Strategy

To develop a reliable RSI algorithm, you need to clearly outline your trading rules, such as:

- Entry Criteria: Define conditions that must be met for a trade to be initiated. For example, an RSI value below 30 might indicate an oversold condition, signaling a potential buy opportunity.

Avery Welles

- Exit Criteria: Determine when to close a trade. You might decide to exit when the RSI crosses above 70, signaling an overbought condition.

- Additional Conditions: You can incorporate other indicators to filter trades, such as moving averages, Bollinger Bands, or price patterns.

Step 2: Writing and Coding the Algorithm

To automate your RSI strategy, you'll need to code it using a trading platform or programming language like Python, MetaTrader, or a broker's proprietary scripting language. Here's a simplified example of an RSI trading script in Python using a library such as `backtrader`:

- Python

```
import backtrader as bt

class RSIStrategy(bt.Strategy):
    def __init__(self):
```

```
    self.rsi = bt.indicators.RSI(period=14)


def next(self):
    if not self.position:
        if self.rsi < 30:
            self.buy()
        elif self.rsi > 70:
            self.sell()
```

This basic code buys when RSI falls below 30 and sells when it rises above 70.

Step 3: Backtesting the Algorithm

Backtesting involves running your strategy on historical market data to evaluate its performance. It helps you identify strengths, weaknesses, and areas for improvement without risking real capital. Important metrics to track during backtesting include:

• Win Rate: The percentage of trades that are profitable.

- Maximum Drawdown: The largest peak-to-trough decline in account balance, indicating potential risk exposure.

- Risk-Reward Ratio: The average reward relative to the risk taken on each trade.

Step 4: Optimizing Parameters

After initial testing, you may need to optimize the parameters of your RSI algorithm. For example, adjusting the RSI period from 14 to 7 or 21 days might yield better results for certain market conditions. Optimization, however, comes with a caveat: be wary of overfitting—making the algorithm too specific to historical data, which can lead to poor performance in real-time markets.

Recommendations

Avery Welles

1. Start with a Simple Strategy: Begin with a basic RSI-based strategy and add complexity gradually as you gain confidence in its performance.

2. Use High-Quality Data: Accurate and comprehensive historical data improves the reliability of backtesting results.

3. Test Across Multiple Market Conditions: Ensure your algorithm performs well in different market environments, including trending and range-bound markets.

Benefits and Pitfalls of Automated RSI Day Trading

1. Elimination of Emotional Bias: Human emotions like fear, greed, and anxiety often lead to poor trading decisions. Automation ensures that trades are executed based on predefined rules, reducing impulsive behavior.

2. Consistency: Automated systems follow their instructions flawlessly, executing trades consistently according to the strategy's logic. This eliminates variability caused by human error or hesitation.

3. Faster Trade Execution: In fast-moving markets, even a slight delay can affect trade outcomes. Algorithms react instantly, capturing opportunities that might be missed by manual traders.

4. 24/7 Market Monitoring: Automated systems can operate continuously, monitoring multiple markets simultaneously and executing trades whenever conditions are met.

5. Backtesting and Optimization: Algorithms can be tested on extensive historical data, providing valuable insights into their performance across various market conditions.

Pitfalls of Automated RSI Day Trading

1. Over-Reliance on Technology: Technical failures, such as connectivity issues or platform crashes, can lead to significant losses. It is crucial to monitor systems periodically and have a contingency plan in place.

2. Overfitting to Historical Data: An over-optimized strategy may perform exceptionally well during backtesting but fail in live trading due to changing market dynamics. Avoid overfitting by using robust testing methodologies and incorporating "out-of-sample" data testing.

3. Market Conditions Change: Automated strategies that work well in one market condition may fail in another. RSI-based systems, for example, may struggle during prolonged trending periods if not adjusted accordingly.

4. Cost and Complexity: Developing and maintaining automated systems requires technical knowledge and, often, financial resources. Custom algorithms may need ongoing adjustments and optimizations.

Recommendations

1. Implement Risk Management Rules: Even with automation, risk controls like position sizing, stop-loss orders, and maximum drawdown limits should be built into your system.

2. Regularly Monitor Performance: Although automated systems reduce hands-on involvement, periodic checks ensure they are functioning correctly and adapting to market conditions.

3. Diversify Your Strategies: Relying solely on one automated strategy can be risky. Consider developing multiple systems tailored to different market conditions.

Using Trading Bots to Enhance Your Strategy

Trading bots—software programs that execute trades based on predefined criteria—are popular among day traders due to their accessibility and versatility.

When integrated with RSI-based strategies, trading bots can help streamline and optimize the trading process.

Types of Trading Bots

1. Signal Bots: These bots generate trade signals based on RSI criteria but do not execute trades automatically. Traders receive alerts and decide whether to act on them.

2. Execution Bots: These bots go a step further, executing trades based on signals generated by the RSI strategy.

3. Arbitrage Bots: While less common in day trading with RSI, these bots seek to exploit price differences across markets or instruments.

4. Market-Making Bots: These bots place both buy and sell orders around the current market price, profiting from the spread.

Customizing and Fine-Tuning Bots for RSI Strategies

To maximize the effectiveness of trading bots with RSI:

- Adjust Bot Parameters: Set bot parameters such as RSI period, overbought/oversold thresholds, and trade size based on your trading strategy and market analysis.

- Combine Indicators: Enhance your bot's decision-making by integrating additional indicators, such as moving averages or Bollinger Bands, alongside RSI.

- Incorporate Risk Management Features: Ensure that your bot includes features like stop-loss orders, trailing stops, and maximum daily loss limits.

Recommendations for Using Trading Bots

1. Use a Reputable Platform: Choose a trustworthy platform or broker that offers robust bot development and testing capabilities.

2. Start with Paper Trading: Test your bot in a simulated environment before deploying it in live markets. This helps you identify any potential issues and refine its performance.

3. Monitor for Unexpected Behavior: Bots can occasionally behave unpredictably due to software glitches or market anomalies. Continuous monitoring ensures that you can intervene if necessary.

By developing and using automated systems, traders can enhance their RSI-based strategies, achieve greater consistency, and take advantage of market opportunities with speed and precision.

Chapter 7

Fine-Tuning and Optimizing Your Strategy

Achieving consistent success in day trading with the Relative Strength Index (RSI) goes beyond simply applying the indicator's core rules. Fine-tuning your strategy to align with market conditions, adapting to shifting trends, and maintaining a continuous improvement process are crucial to building long-term profitability.

Identifying Market Conditions for RSI Success

To maximize the effectiveness of RSI-based strategies, understanding the market conditions in which RSI thrives

Avery Welles

is essential. The RSI is particularly well-suited for identifying overbought and oversold levels, trend strength, and potential reversals. However, it performs differently across various market environments, and being able to distinguish when and how to use it can significantly impact results.

Trending vs. Range-Bound Markets

One of the most critical factors in the success of any RSI strategy is the distinction between trending and range-bound (sideways) markets:

- Trending Markets: In strong upward or downward trends, RSI signals can be misleading. For example, an asset might remain in overbought territory during a prolonged uptrend or oversold during a sustained downtrend. In these situations, RSI-based traders often utilize higher thresholds, such as 80/20 instead of the standard 70/30 levels, to reduce false signals.

- Range-Bound Markets: In a market moving sideways with well-defined support and resistance levels, RSI is highly effective for pinpointing entry and exit points. Buy signals occur when RSI indicates oversold conditions, while sell signals occur during overbought conditions.

Confirming Market Conditions

Identifying market conditions is the first step toward effective strategy optimization. Some helpful tools for distinguishing trends include:

- Moving Averages: The relationship between short-term and long-term moving averages can provide context for trend strength and direction. For instance, if a 50-day moving average is above a 200-day moving average, the market is generally considered bullish.

- ADX (Average Directional Index): This indicator quantifies trend strength. A low ADX (below 25) suggests a range-bound market, while a high ADX (above 25) indicates a trending market.

Adapting to Changing Market Trends

Markets are dynamic, and strategies that work in one environment may falter in another. Adapting your RSI-based strategy to changing market conditions requires flexibility, vigilance, and a willingness to modify your approach as needed.

Recognizing Shifts in Market Behavior

Market trends can change due to economic data releases, geopolitical events, or shifts in investor sentiment. Some key signs that indicate a market transition include:

- Increased Volatility: A sudden surge in price fluctuations may signal that the market is transitioning from a range-bound state to a trending state or vice versa.

- Breakouts and Breakdowns: The breakout of a key support or resistance level often marks the beginning of a new trend.

- Changes in Volume: An increase in trading volume can indicate growing market interest and may precede a trend change.

Adapting RSI Strategies for Changing Conditions

1. Adjust Timeframes: In fast-moving markets, consider shortening the RSI calculation period to capture quicker movements. Conversely, lengthen the period during calmer markets for a more stable signal.

2. Dynamic Stop-Loss and Take-Profit Levels: Alter your stop-loss and take-profit points to reflect changing volatility. Tight stops work well during low-volatility periods, while wider stops may be needed in more volatile environments.

3. Switch Between Strategies: Have multiple RSI strategies prepared for different market conditions. For example, a countertrend strategy for range-bound markets and a trend-following strategy for strong trends.

Keeping a Trading Journal and Improving Performance

A trading journal is a powerful tool for improving your RSI-based trading strategy. It provides insights into what works, what doesn't, and how your strategy performs under different conditions. By maintaining a detailed journal, you can track your trades, review your decisions, and identify areas for improvement.

Key Elements of a Trading Journal

1. Trade Details: Record essential details for each trade, including entry and exit points, position size, stop-loss levels, and reasons for entering/exiting.

2. Market Context: Note the prevailing market conditions, such as trend direction, volatility, and any relevant news or events.

3. Strategy Used: Specify the exact RSI strategy you employed, including thresholds, timeframes, and any complementary indicators.

4. Trade Outcome: Record the result of the trade, including profit or loss, and analyze why it succeeded or failed.

Using the Journal to Optimize Your Strategy

1. Identify Patterns in Success and Failure: Look for recurring themes in your successful and unsuccessful trades. For example, do you perform better in range-bound markets? Does high volatility lead to more losses?

2. Refine Entry and Exit Rules: Use your trading history to fine-tune your entry and exit criteria. Perhaps waiting for an additional confirmation signal before entering would reduce false signals.

3. Set Performance Goals: Define specific, measurable goals based on your journal's insights. For instance, you might aim to improve your win rate by 5% over the next month by adjusting your stop-loss strategy.

Example of a Trading Journal Entry

- Date: January 15, 2024
- Market Condition: Trending up, high volatility
- RSI Strategy: Entered long when RSI crossed 35 from below in a pullback; exit set at RSI reaching 65
- Entry/Exit Points: Entered at $50, exited at $57
- Position Size: 100 shares
- Stop-Loss: $48
- Outcome: +$700
- Notes: Good trade, but anxiety during pullback before reaching exit signal. Consider smaller position size in volatile markets.

By fine-tuning your RSI strategy, adapting to changing market trends, and maintaining a detailed trading journal, you can achieve a higher level of discipline, flexibility, and performance in your day trading endeavors.

Avery Welles

Avery Welles

Conclusion

As we reach the end of 'Day Trading with Relative Strength Index (RSI)', it's time to reflect on the journey you've embarked upon. This book has aimed to guide you through the intricate world of day trading, equipping you with deep insights into leveraging one of the market's most versatile and powerful indicators—RSI. But knowledge alone does not lead to success; it's the disciplined application, continuous learning, and adaptation that ultimately separates successful traders from the rest.

From exploring the foundations of RSI, delving into its origins, and learning its calculation intricacies, we laid the groundwork for understanding the true potential and limitations of this tool. We compared RSI with other indicators, debunked myths, and highlighted its unique advantages. Understanding how to wield RSI effectively within the broader context of market movements and technical indicators was a key focus, ensuring you can make well-informed trading decisions.

Our exploration of advanced techniques took the core principles of RSI to new heights, offering strategies like multi-timeframe analysis, integrations with other key indicators, and fine-tuning parameters for maximum precision. Whether navigating sideways markets or riding trends, you now have a toolkit capable of evolving alongside shifting market conditions.

As you move forward, let this book serve as a living reference and companion on your trading journey. Day trading is both an art and a science, and mastering it requires patience, perseverance, and a commitment to lifelong learning. While market conditions may change, the fundamentals of preparation, discipline, and strategy refinement remain timeless.

I hope that through this book, you have gained a comprehensive understanding of RSI's transformative potential and how it can fit into your trading arsenal. May it guide you to achieve consistent gains, navigate market turbulence with confidence, and make informed decisions with clarity and precision.

Wishing you success in your trading endeavors and beyond. Keep learning, stay adaptable, and trade wisely. The market is your canvas, and with the right tools, you can create a masterpiece of consistent success. Happy trading!